Pay My Mortgage!

Miss Sue Hoyuela

Pay My Mortgage!

ISBN-13: 978-1468147537

DEDICATION

This book is dedicated to my husband, Jaime who has been the world's greatest partner and host. And to all those who have stayed with us and left their footprints on our lives.

Blessings to you all!

Pay My Mortgage!

CONTENTS

Pay My Mortgage!

1 NOT JUST ANOTHER "WORK AT HOME" JOB

Congratulations! You are reading this because you are open to making money not just by *working from home*, but by *using your home* to make extra money. Now your commute to work is the equivalent of rolling out of bed and walking to the coffee maker. Now a portion of your home and utility bills are a write off. Now you can get paid to do the things you regularly do anyways, like clean the house and do laundry. What could be better?

Imagine getting paid while sharing a cup of tea with a nice lady from Australia, or perhaps giving directions to a young couple from Germany who would like to enjoy an evening on the town, or even while watching television or puttering in your garden.

Making extra money with your home is actually a much easier, less time consuming way of making money than on the internet, assembling products, stuffing envelopes, secret shopping, etc., and much more rewarding, in my opinion.

I have been able to make the same amount of money *using my home* in just ten hours <u>per month</u> as I earned in a full month at my regular job as a manager. It did not take long before I did the math and decided to fire my boss. Take it from me, freedom is wonderful and I want that for you. Now the question you have to ask yourself is, "Do I want that for me?" If your answer was a resounding, "Yes!" then let me show you how you can create stress free income and financial freedom for yourself.

Through this book you will be introduced to the wonderful world of hosting and a brand new website that makes financial freedom possible. You are provided with a free website to showcase your space so that you can reach a worldwide audience. The opportunities that this provides are mindblowing.

This website provides the means through which travelers and hosts can communicate. In return, you pay a small percentage whenever a transaction goes through. There are no monthly subscription fees. You only pay when you get paid first. Brilliant!.

2 COMING TO TERMS WITH HAVING STRANGERS IN YOUR HOUSE

Everyone we know says we're crazy. The one question I get asked more than anything else is, "But isn't it scary having strangers in your house?" The honest truth is that it is a huge blessing. The people we meet are so kind and wonderful and have the most adventurous spirits. I have found that I learn something new from each guest and I am richer for it. But if you will indulge me, I would like to share some background on how we came to be involved in hosting and a true story about some friends that were particularly special to us.

My husband and I have been hosting people in our home since 1992. It began innocently enough. A relative from Mexico wanted to come to the United States to study. She needed a place to stay while going to school so she lived with us for 2 years, got her degree and returned home. Then another relative from Mexico needed to buy a car. He believed that he could get a better deal in the U.S. so he slept on our sofa for 2 weeks while he aggressively searched for and found his dream car. He was so focused on his goal and driven (pun intended) to succeed that he was able to hunt down the perfect car on time and under budget. It was a satisfied man who revved up the engine of his 1985 Mustang and drove off into the sunset.

A few months later we were at church and the pastor announced that a large seminar was to be held at our church. Pastors were being flown in from all around the world to attend the week-long event and the congregation was asked if anyone could provide a bed or two for some of the out of town guests. My husband and I said, "Why not?" So we were blessed to host two Australian pastors for the most memorable week of our lives. They were crazy and fun-loving people so we woke them up in the morning by playing the song, "Macarena". It works better than an alarm clock! They jumped right out of bed and started doing the dance right along with us.

One of the pastors brought us a beautiful emu egg that had been laid by one of his own emus on his farm back in Australia. The egg had been cleaned and polished to a deep turquoise blue by his son. It was displayed on a hand-carved wooden base that he had made himself from a native Australian tree grown on his own property. An engraved gold plate was affixed to the wooden base with his name, and the city he was from. He made it with the intention of giving it to his hosts as a way of thanking them for their hospitality and opening up their home to him. I imagined the long hours he had spent carefully creating this gift for strangers, strangers who would later become like family. It was the most thoughtful gift I had ever received and it brought tears to my eyes.

I believe that experience helped open our hearts to the possibility of hosting on a permanent basis.

A little while later we heard from a friend that a local university had a need for host families. The university offered an English language program that attracted students from all around the world. Students would come for as short as two weeks or as long as nine months to learn or improve their English language skills. For many students, it was an opportunity to increase their earning potential back home by showing their command of the English language. We began partnering with the university as a host family in 1998.

Our experiences with the hosting program were varied and positive. The youngest student we hosted was a 14-year-old boy from China. The oldest was also from China; a 65 year old gentleman. He was definitely young at heart though because he chose to sleep on the top bunk! I could go on for days (and pages for that matter) with great stories of experiences we have shared and life-long friendships we have made. But let me highlight the story of Ricardo and Mayumi. (Names shared with permission).

Ricardo came to us from Ecuador. He was twenty years old at the time and had previously learned English, surprisingly enough, by staying at a Kibbutz in Israel for nine months. When he came to America to improve his English and to stay at our house, he quickly learned that our neighborhood was primarily Hispanic. The irony was not lost on him when he went to the grocery store and asked for help to find an item. The sales girl didn't understand when he spoke to her in English. Instead she responded in his native language, Spanish! "What did I come here for then?!" Ricardo exclaimed. He was later to discover that it was written in the stars.

Ricardo continued to attend his English classes and quickly mastered the language. He was a bright, energetic and charismatic young man who drew people to him naturally. He would arrange impromptu soccer games and trips to the beach and have a mob ready to participate at a moment's notice.

During that same period of time, we had another student staying with us named Shotaro. Shotaro was a young man in his early twenties from Japan who was a little shy. He and Ricardo would drive to school together and shared many of the same classes. Over lunch one day Ricardo pointed out a beautiful Japanese girl across the room. He said, "Shotaro, why don't you go and talk to her?" Shotaro shook his head and smiled bashfully. "No, I couldn't do that," he said.

That evening, Ricardo was telling us about the Japanese girl that they had seen at school and that Shotaro and she would be perfect together. My husband, who is a match-maker at heart, quickly challenged Ricardo with this, "I bet you $10 that you can't get her to come to dinner at our house tomorrow night." Ricardo, with a gleam in his eye, shook his hand confidently and said, "I'll take that bet!" Shotaro didn't seem to mind that they were conspiring together.

The next evening we had company for dinner. Ricardo was smiling from ear to ear as he introduced us to our dinner guest, Mayumi. My husband arranged for Shotaro and Mayumi to make us an authentic Japenese dish together for dinner that night and then they were strategically seated at the dinner table as well. However, Shotaro mostly stared at his plate the whole evening and ate silently. Surprisingly though, there was definitely a spark of attraction between Ricardo and Mayumi.

Well, the rest is history. After that night Ricardo and Mayumi began dating. When school ended and they had to return to their home countries, they continued their long distance relationship. Ricardo finished school with his engineering degree and then moved to Japan to be with Mayumi. Their courtship lasted four years until they were finally married, in Guam. Shotaro was the best man at their wedding.

I could fill a book with stories of laughter, love, fun and so many amazing experiences that we have had simply because we opened our hearts and our home to hosting people from around the world. They may have started out as strangers but became family as soon as we greeted them at our door.

Now I ask you this very important question, do you think you are ready for financial freedom through hosting? Before you decide, know that you are not saying that you are willing to let just anybody into your home. You are in full control over who you allow to stay with you and it is always okay to say, "no". So, with that in mind, if you are ready to proceed, then read on and I will walk with you step by step through getting started and setting up your free website that is the gateway to the wonderful world of hosting.

To your success!

3 TARGETING YOUR IDEAL GUEST

Know Your Market

Congratulations! You are ready to begin renting out a room or rooms in your house. Before we dive right in, you must start by asking yourself this very important question: "What type of people am I comfortable having in my home?" This is particularly important if you are also living in the home and will be sharing common spaces such as the living room, kitchen and/or restroom, or even if you have a separate rental property.

Think about the type of people you would like to attract. Perhaps you enjoy families with children. If you like it quiet, then specify the age range you prefer. If you have a large house, you could open it up to groups who need a place for a party or a baby shower. The possibilities are endless.

"Couch surfing" is quite popular these days for people who are traveling for months at a time. It can be quite economical for them and quite profitable for you.

There are many reasons that people may be looking for a place to stay. Some are on vacation. Some are on business. Some are going to school. Some want to relocate. Some are looking for a place long-term. Some may even want to stay just for a few hours to catch a nap before moving on to their next destination.

Travelers often prefer staying in people's homes because it affords them a cheaper alternative to a hotel. Plus, houses come with fully equipped kitchens, which you don't normally find in hotel rooms. If you have other amenities such as wireless internet, a washer and dryer, a hot tub, breakfast included, horses, etc., those can make your home even more attractive and great selling points to help target a certain type of guest.

You've heard the saying, "Location, location, location"? You may be thinking that your dwelling place is in an undesirable area. Well, that is not necessarily true. You may be located in the country or on the outskirts of a town. That might appeal to people who enjoy dirt bike riding, hiking, horseback riding or all manner of outdoor activities. In fact, there is a huge "Eco-Tour" movement going on now for people who are looking for more excitement in their vacations. You could offer an outdoor experience package that would appeal to this ever-growing portion of the population.

The word "Eco" is also being tacked onto words to mean earth-friendly. People are looking for ways to reduce their impact on the earth which can be demonstrated through recycling, eating a vegan diet, or even living in a perma-culture society.

My point is this; do not say, "no" for people. Put your offer out there and let them decide. I am willing to bet that you will be surprised by the overwhelmingly positive response from people who want to pay to stay at your place.

Describing your Ideal Guest

Another important aspect is to consider not only who your perfect guest would be but also what type of guest would enjoy what you have to offer. Shortly you will be writing a description of your ideal guest and making a list of attributes. I want you to really get those creative juices flowing to think about what is unique about your place and the type of people that would enjoy it most. But before we do that, here is one more little exercise. Go to the following website: www.airbnb.com. On the main page is a single question, "Where do you want to go?" Beside it you will see a slide show of all kinds of places for rent. Just watch as the pictures scroll by. You will see mansions, cabins, couches, castles, tree houses, yachts and everything in between. I want you to expand your mind to the possibilities of what you can rent out. The message here is that the unique, the unusual, the quaint and eclectic are all very attractive as well as the traditional. Essentially, there is no wrong way to break into this industry.

Now, with that in mind make two lists, one with at least 10 words describing your ideal guest and a second detailing what is unique about your place, your space, that would appeal to your ideal guest.

Put these lists side by side and see how they line up. Keep these lists handy because we will be using them when we write your Description.

4 GETTING PAID, SAFETY AND SECURITY

You are probably saying, "Hold on a minute there, Miss Sue. I still have a couple of questions before I jump in to the deep end with this. First of all, how do I get paid? Second of all, how do I know that I will be safe? And how about my things, what if they get stolen or damaged?"

Collecting the Money

Be encouraged that hosting is a fun and profitable way to make money from home. When you set up your free website through a neutral trustworthy third party, they handle the financial side of the transaction. When the guest books your room, they pay upfront with a credit card to hold the room. Their money is held for you until the day after the guests check in. The money is then directly deposited to your account. This method of using a trustworthy middle man means that:

- You are assured of payment

- You do not have to approach your guests directly about payment.

- Guests can pay in any currency and you do not have to worry about conversion rates and fees.

- Guests can pay by credit card and you do not have to worry about having a merchant account and paying fees.

- 24-hour Customer Support is available for any questions.

Now that all of the financial worries are taken care of, you are free to enjoy your guests.

Screening

You've heard it said, "Life is like a box of chocolates, you never know what you are going to get." Well, we have ways of helping you sort out the nuts to keep you safe and secure. Before a guest can book your room, you first receive an email "Inquiry" and a lot of helpful information about them. When they request to stay with you, they must provide a picture of themselves. If they look alright to you, go ahead and click on their picture which will take you to a brief profile summary of who they are, what they are about and why they are traveling. They must provide a reason for their trip as well as the dates they want to stay and the number of people that will be in their party. You will also be able to see how long they have been a member of the community as well as how many Facebook friends they have along with other verifications such as their phone number and social media status. Best of all, if they have stayed with other hosts, you can read the reviews to see if they were well behaved or not.

This is your chance to have a conversation with your potential guest, to be sure you feel comfortable. You have three ways you can respond: Accept, Decline, or Request More Information. Feel free to take as much time and ask as many questions as you need. And remember, it is always okay to say no.

Security

When it comes to security, a $1,000,000 host protection guarantee covers you for any loss from vandalism or theft.

You are now free to enjoy all of the benefits of hosting, with none of the worries.

5 BEFORE YOU LIST YOUR PLACE, PREPARE THE SPACE

Now that we have addressed all of your concerns and you are indeed ready to jump in with both feet, let's begin by preparing the space that will be perfect for your ideal guest. This is where your list will come in handy as we begin to think through what will make them most comfortable.

But before I go on with the practical points, please indulge me and join me in a philosophical meditation. Just for a moment, let's think about what it is to be human. Isn't it strange that human beings have a physical need to shut down, turn off if you will, every eighteen hours or so? I am speaking of course, of sleeping. Our bodies are prone, lax, vulnerable during those six to eight hours (on average) while the body goes into a state of unconsciousness and recharges itself. We want to leave our bodies in a safe, comfortable place while this cycle is running so that it can get the greatest benefit from this rest and also not be harmed in any way. Strangely enough, this odd habit of having to rest and recharge periodically creates a need that we as hosts can fill. Isn't that wonderful?

So practically speaking, this means our guests' basic needs are for a clean, bug-free bed, that would ideally but not necessarily be in a room that can be made dark, quiet and a comfortable temperature.

The ability for the guest to lock the door also provides a stress-free environment. That should be simple enough.

So let's start with the most important feature: the bed.

Guests generally focus on their comfort first and will begin by checking the mattress or couch cushions for springiness. They do not want springs poking them. They want a minimum amount of squeaking. And the mattress must not be too soft nor too firm. Often, there is not much you can do if the firmness of the bed is not to their liking. However, I have found that any mattress benefits from an additional pillow-top cover.

You've heard the phrase, "Good night. Sleep tight. Don't let the bed bugs bite." Well, believe me, in this business you need to take this very seriously. Guests will look for signs of creepy crawlies, stains, or evidence of the previous occupant of the bed. Let there be no such evidence, lest the guest leave a bad review or demand a refund.

The sheets should be clean and stain-free as well as the comforter and other blankets that are provided.

Twin beds are my size of choice. They can be arranged in a myriad of ways to accommodate groups of many sizes. It just depends on how many you can comfortably squeeze into a room. I avoid headboards and bed frames when at all possible.

They add a level of difficulty when arranging a room for different numbers of guests and they cause a safety issue when people bang their shins on the sharp corners. If your ideal guest is easy going and just needs a no-frills place to sleep at night, a box spring and mattress on the floor will usually be just fine.

People generally prefer to sleep in a dark and quiet space and within a comfortable temperature range. As hosts we always look for ways to provide extra value for our guests. Make sure the room has curtains or window blinds to block out excess light. You could even offer a sleep mask and ear plugs to ensure that your guest's sleep is uninterrupted.

Provide a key to the room as well. The guest will sleep more securely and be able to leave their belongings in a safe place when they venture out.

A comfortable room should also contain a desk with a lamp, a chair and a dresser. Depending on your target market, these things may not be critical, especially if you are just renting a couch or an airbed on your living room floor. This is where your knowledge of your ideal guest will come in to play and you can plan for their comforts accordingly.

However, let me point out that these days wireless internet (wifi) is an extremely important amenity to provide and it can make or break the deal when a guest is making a decision of where to stay

6 ADDING THE SIZZLE

So now that we have the basic needs met, let's add the sizzle. In real estate, a house is sometimes described as having, "curb appeal". That means that if you were to simply drive by the house, you would fall in love with it just because it looked so perfect. This appeal is usually achieved by adding cosmetic touches such as flower boxes, fresh paint or the proverbial white picket fence.

We want to apply this same method of enhancement to the space you will be renting so that it will appeal to your ideal guest. This is where we get to have some fun.

The easiest and most economical way to liven up a room is to paint it. With paint you can give a room a facelift, make it look bright, alive and clean, and change the look and feel in an instant.

You can also create a theme. If you live in Maine, use a lobster motif. If you live in Hawaii, decorate with palm trees. If you live in California, hang a picture of the Hollywood sign on the wall. If you have several rooms available to rent, you can create a different theme for each one such as "The Cave Room" which could be decorated with stone, rock, marble, etc. Or you could have "The Zen Room" for quiet and relaxation in an Asian style with a small indoor fountain, a Zen garden with sand, rocks and a rake, rice paper screens and candles.

Perhaps a jungle theme would be fun. You can do so much with blankets, comforters, rugs and pictures.

When we add sizzle we always need to keep two things in mind. The first is to not get too carried away. Sizzle can be expensive so let me give you a rule of thumb. Whatever you spend to get the room setup, let it cost less then what you plan to make each month, which is something we will discuss in a later chapter. As with any business, there are always startup costs. But we want to limit those costs so that our business can start generating a net profit as soon as possible. Therefore, let's keep the expenses low or even spread them out over time by adding enhancements gradually.

The second thing is to be sure that we are adding value to our guest's stay, not to our own. That may seem strange to say but we often get in our own way and add things that we like, but the guest may not necessarily appreciate. To share a story from my own experience, one time I thought it would be nice to provide a refrigerator in the room for my guests. It turned out that the noise from the motor bothered them so much that guest after guest kept unplugging it. They actually preferred to share some space in our main refrigerator and we eventually removed the personal fridge altogether. The refrigerator became a non-value-added feature and we would have done better to save the money and apply it elsewhere. Lesson learned.

The key here is to be strategic in the amenities we provide by putting ourselves in our guests' shoes and seeing the experience from their perspective. For example, let's say that your ideal guest is a 23-year-old male who is backpacking around the world. You might want to provide an ironing board and an iron for him, but chances are, he will have very little use for them. However, if you were to put a map of the local area on the desk along with bus schedules and a discount coupon to a local attraction, that would be something that could make his trip more memorable and fun; something he would definitely appreciate.

7 STAGING & PHOTOGRAPHY

Now that we have the room all set up and ready for your guests, we need to let them know it is there. We will start by taking some nice digital pictures. But, before we start clicking away, let's first do some staging. That simply means arranging things in an attractive manner so that the space will look its best. There are a few tips and tricks to it however.

Rule #1: No clutter! Remove any debris that is lying around that does not belong. This includes cleaning so that things will sparkle. You'd be surprised how much folks can see in pictures today, what with the zoom feature and all. You don't want any negative details to detract from the positive impression you are making.

Rule #2: Straighten, organize and align. That means folding blankets neatly, straightening cushions, centering knick knacks on shelves or table tops, and making sure pictures are not crooked.

Rule #3: Add some color. You can put a vase of fresh flowers on the coffee table, or a bowl of fresh fruit on the dining table, or maybe a platter of fresh baked goods. Hang a colorful blanket over the back of a sofa, chair or the foot of the bed.

Rule #4: Add items to make the space look more inviting. This is where we have a bit of fun. To do this, first imagine you are your ideal guest and you are using that space. What would you be doing while you are enjoying it the most?

Let's say for example you have a beautiful 4-post bed in a lovely room. Through your pictures you want your guest to be able to imagine themselves in that room and enjoying that room. What if you were to turn on the bedside lamp and place an opened book face down on the table beside the lamp? This suggests, ever-so-subtly, that when the guest stays, they might relax with a good book before going to sleep. And might I suggest a plate of cookies with a cold glass of milk on the bedside table as well? You might laugh, but trust me, it works.

Or if you have a breakfast nook area, you might set out a coffee mug and strategically arrange an opened newspaper to set the mood. What are you saying with this photo? "Start your morning with a fresh hot cup of coffee in a quiet, comfortable setting."

Set out a board game on a coffee table that looks like someone has been playing it to make families feel welcome.

Set up a croquet game on the lawn and lean a couple of bicycles against the wall in the background to suggest that the great outdoors beckons them to come and relax and play.

Or, my personal favorite; set up a lounge chair beside the pool with a nice beach towel covering it.

On a small table beside the lounge chair, place an ice bucket with ice inside (this creates a nice effect with the condensation trickling down the sides of the bucket). Wrap a bottle of Martinelli's Sparkling Apple Juice in a white linen towel to give the illusion that it is a bottle of champagne and put it in the bucket. Set a wine glass on the table beside the bucket and perhaps a pair of sunglasses. Now imagine yourself in that setting. Ah, pure bliss.

Now you are ready to start taking pictures. Position yourself in such a way as to capture the primary components that tell a story. By the way, feel free to take as many pictures as you need to. You can zoom out and take a picture of the whole room, then come in close to focus on each specific area of that room, go for it. Remember that you are telling a story through your pictures and you want it to speak volumes!

But wait a minute. I have overlooked something very important. What if you are thinking, "I'm not a good photographer"? "I don't have a good camera." "I have a camera on my phone, but it doesn't even come with a flash." Well, not to worry. I have good news for you, my friend. For select areas, a professional photographer can come out to your place and take pictures for you for free! Yes, that's right. They will also touch up the photos so as to present your space in the absolute best light. Amazing, but true. Photography appointments can be set up through your website. A professional photographer will truly do your space justice in digital photos. Plus, you will have a special "verified" flag on your photos to give you that much needed credibility in the eyes of your potential guests. And that's a good thing.

For now though, we will go ahead and use the photos you have taken because you need to upload at least one profile picture of yourself and one listing picture in order to get started. We do not want to delay your website's launch at this point. Don't worry, you can always add the professional pictures later.

8 CREATING YOUR PROFILE

Let's get started on creating your very own webpage for free that will drive traffic to your space for rent.

But first, we will need to setup your account.

Go to the website: www.airbnb.com. Click on the link at the top, "Sign Up".

Click on the link at the top of the next page; "Create an account using my e-mail address"

You may choose to connect through your Facebook account (if you have one), or just through your main email account.

One of the secrets to airbnb's success is the verification feature. The more verifications each person has, the safer the community becomes. Go ahead and set up as many verification as you can by verifying your email, your phone number, your twitter account, your linkedin account and requesting references from your friends.

Next you will need to upload your Profile Picture. Don't worry, this doesn't have to be a glamour shot, just something where you are recognizable so when the guest shows up at your door, they feel like they know you already.

If you would like to record a video greeting, you can do that too. It's up to you, whatever you feel more comfortable with.

Here, you will also choose how you want to get paid. My personal preference is Paypal. If you already have a Paypal account, you can receive payments simply by providing your email account that is linked to it. You can then connect your Paypal account to your bank account to transfer your money for free.

Now that your Profile is complete, let's go ahead and set up your listing.

.

9 CREATING YOUR LISTING

Uploading Photos

Now we are ready to get down to the nitty gritty. Begin creating your listing by uploading the pictures that you took of the house and the guest room. Keep in mind that the photo in the first position will be the main photo that is displayed in searches. Be sure to make it a good one. This is the photo that sells the sizzle.

Editing Photos

Click over to the "Edit" tab to arrange the photos and add captions. Simply click in the white box near the bottom of the photo and type your description. When you are done, click on the "Save" button. Continue to add catchy captions to all of your photos in this manner. You can rearrange the order of the pictures later if you like so that they will tell a story and take the potential guest on a virtual tour of your place when they are scrolling through the pictures.

Title

Next, let's go to the Description. You will first need to add a Title for the room/space you are renting. Do your best to add the most common keywords that your ideal guest would be searching on to find you. This is your chance to optimize how your listing comes up in searches. Whatever words you use in your title, use them again as the first words in your description. This will help your page to come up higher in search engines such as Google, Bing and Yahoo.

Description

In your description you are shooting for at least 250 words so use this opportunity to speak to your ideal guest in "their language" by including all of the features that they are looking for. You want their heart to race when they see your pictures and read the description because they will be thinking, "By god, I think I've found it! This is the place I've been looking for!"

Talk about the space you are renting. Does it have a bed? If so, describe how comfortable it is, how clean, how quiet, the thread count of the sheets, etc.

The restroom is always a critical issue. How close is it to the sleeping area? Is it a private bathroom, or will it be shared with others? Is it a full bathroom?

A full bathroom includes the toilet, sink and a shower with a bath tub. A ¾ bath includes a toilet, sink and a shower. A ½ bath includes a toilet and a sink only.

What amenities come with it? A refrigerator, a microwave, a private entrance, wireless internet.

Be sure to be completely honest by mentioning any potential detractors for guests such as pets (many people are allergic to animal dander) or if there are smokers in the house. You can say it in a positive way by saying that smoking is allowed in your home, or by including cute pictures of your pets and introducing them as the other members of your family. It is better to disclose everything up front rather than to have a disgruntled guest leave a bad review.

Local attractions. Now is the time to throw in keywords. Keep in mind that your description will be posted on the internet. People will be searching on keywords to find what they are looking for and you want them to find you. Think about what attracts people to your area. Are there any amusement parks nearby? If so, feel free to drop some big names like, Disneyland, The Mall of America or Six Flags. Do people come for the museums, the outdoor experiences, the clubs? Throw in things like, "The Museum of Contemporary Art (M.O.C.A.)", "swim with the dolphins", or "the hottest jazz club east of the Mississippi!"

Perhaps they are in the area for business more often than not. If so, make sure your rates are comparable to or lower than the local hotels so you can attract guests by offering a "home away from home" and possibly throw in free parking and/or a free breakfast.

As you are writing your description, always be completely honest. As a host, you are reviewed by your guests after each stay and one of the 6 categories that you are rated on is "Accuracy". Potential guests reading your listing will expect you to provide what has been promised. We are also obligated to provide hot water and working appliances. Guests have a right to ask for a refund if anything is not as promised or appliances aren't working. So be careful to check the right boxes and if anything should change, update your listing right away.

When writing your description, provide as much value as you can. Let your potential guests know that your goal is to blow them away with amazing service and demonstrate that you are actively looking for ways to enhance their experience. Believe me, it will be rewarding in more ways than one.

Amenities

Once your description is complete, scroll down and check the boxes in front of the Amenities that apply.

Details

After completing the Amenities section, scroll down to the Details section. Under the "Accommodates" drop down menu, you will enter the maximum number of guests that you are willing to have in that space at one time. Next, fill in the number of bedrooms. Even if you have more than one bedroom that you are renting out, always put 1 here. You should create a separate listing for each room/space that you have. This is necessary for keeping track of the calendar later on and you will be able to set different prices for each space if you like.

Now, thinking of this particular room that you are describing, accurately select the number of beds and then the type of beds that are offered in that room. The type of beds will fall into one of the following categories: Airbed, Couch, Futon, Pull-out sofa, or Real Bed.

Next list the number of bathrooms available and the square footage (more or less) of the space the guest will be renting.

The House Manual

Writing the House Manual can be very helpful. The House Manual is a different document, one that will only be revealed to guests who actually book a reservation. This is the next step in making the guest feel welcome and comfortable. You are probably wondering, "What should I write in the House Manual? I've already written a 250-word description. Isn't that enough?"

Imagine that the House Manual is your voice introducing your guests to your place in a virtual tour *after they have arrived*. To get an idea, have a friend pretend to be a new guest and you are welcoming them at your door. What might you say? "Hello! Please come in and make yourself at home."

You might let them know that one of your customs is to not wear shoes in the house and point out the best place to leave them. You might describe how to work the washer and dryer. Your place might have some little quirks that the guest should know about such as a door handle that sticks so you have to push really hard to open it. After you have toured a few guests through your house, you will find yourself mentioning the same things each time. Those are the things you can put in your House Manual.

You can also let the guests know about any rules you have about curfew or the appropriate smoking area, where to leave the key when they check out or the best place to park. Warn them of any permits needed or restricted parking areas. They will appreciate the advice.

The hard part is that when we live in a place for a while, we begin to take things for granted. Do a little exercise for me. Look around your place and imagine that you are seeing it for the first time. When giving a new guest a tour, feel free to state things that may seem obvious to you, such as which way to turn the hot water faucet on and off. As you host more and more people from around the world, you will begin to discover that people from other cultures can have customs that differ from your own in surprising ways.

The House Manual will continue to evolve as your experience grows. As you listen to your guests' questions, continue to add the answers to the House Manual like a FAQ (Frequently Asked Questions) sheet.

Pets

Next, be sure to check the proper box in front of "pets" or "no pets".

Location

The next section is labeled, "Location". This shows a map of your neighborhood and a flag for your exact location. Do not worry, this information will only be provided to people who have already secured their booking and paid. After booking, a guest's first question is usually, "Now how do I get to your place?" They can either choose to follow the map provided on the website, or simply enter the address in their GPS or give it to the cab driver. There is also a section for you to type in directions if you like. Remember, you can never add too much value or detail so feel free to provide the new guest with as much information as possible. It will put their mind at ease and lower their stress level when traveling to a new place.

Right below the "Location" section is a "Public View" section. This is what is shown to potential guests who want to get an idea of where you live, but the actual address is not yet provided for your safety. I recommend setting it at, "Nearby" which gives a two-block radius which is good enough for folks to use to determine how far away your location is from their desired points of interest.

Once you have all of this information completed to your satisfaction, click on the "Save" button.

Good job!

9 SETTING THE PRICE

Now it is time to look at the business aspect of Your hosting endeavor. I know you would probably host people in your home just because it is so enriching to meet new people from all corners of the globe. Building strong relationships after all, is its own reward. But add the fun of regularly adding funds to your bank account, and now we have something that is not just rewarding personally, but also financially.

Setting the price is a bit of an art form but I have found a formula for success that is a sure fire way to make money right off the bat.

As you enter this new and uncharted territory, proceed cautiously. Get to know the natives and let them get to know you a bit. What do I mean by this? Well, when you first post your listing on the website, you will have no credibility. Credibility comes with time as you accumulate good reviews and establish yourself as a super host. For the first few months you will be bending over backwards to get great reviews by wowing your guests through quality and service while keeping everything clean and pristine. And, you will be doing all this at the lowest price that you can bear. As the saying goes, "short term pain for long term gain." By pricing your place lower than anybody else's, guests will flock to you. Once you have a slew of good reviews under your belt, then you can go ahead and ease the price up. We will give it at least a good three months to establish your reputation so that guests will know that paying a higher price will be worth it, especially when they read your rave reviews.

That being said, let's start with a little market research. Go onto the website and search on your city and state. Sort the listings: "Price: low to high".

Take a look at the other listings that are competing for guests in your area. Take note of how many reviews they have. See if they are positive. Note how many stars they have received in the 6 critical categories: Accuracy, Cleanliness, Check in, Communication, Location and Value. Notice the host's response time for inquiries. Pay attention to how detailed their description is and how many pictures they have posted. Whatever the competition is doing, you can either learn from them and do what they do (why reinvent the wheel after all?) or go over and beyond what they are doing to win more guests to your location.

Most importantly, check to see what the lowest price is and what the guest gets for that price. A good starting price is usually $25 per night. If you want to undercut the competition to get started, you might try $20 per night, but as a rule, don't go below $10 per night. If you are priced low enough, you will receive a lot of responses which in turn can boost your Response Rating. Your Response Rating tracks how many inquiries you respond to and how quickly you respond. You should strive to keep your rating at 95% or above. I recommend getting a cell phone with internet and email. That way you can always be ready to respond to inquiries wherever you are. Please note that this frees you up to be able to make money from anywhere, not just at home in front of your computer. Bonus!

So, let's just say that you have decided to start out by charging $25 per night. If there are an average of 30 nights in a month, the potential monthly income for that room would be $750.

Stop right there. Let me ask you this. How much can you typically rent a room for to a regular tenant in your area? You can easily find ads in your local newspaper for rooms for rent to get an idea of what they go for. I can tell you this though, in my neighborhood there is no way the market would bear $750 per month for just one room in a house. This is a case where the parts are worth more than the whole. If you have more than one room to rent, you can multiply this $750 per month times as many rooms as you can spare. Heck, create spaces to rent if you have to. This can become a goldmine!

Keep in mind that this is our teaser rate, the starting point to just get the guests in for the first three months or so. After you have several strong reviews, then you will be able to start gently bumping the price up until it is at the highest price the market will bear.

So let's talk about the best way to set up the pricing for your space. Go to the "Pricing and Terms" section of the website and enter the dollar figure you have settled on as your beginning "Nightly" rate. You will notice that when you enter that rate in the "Nightly" box and tab out of it, a suggested range will appear beside the "Weekly" and "Monthly" boxes. If we do the math, we discover that these rates would give a price break to the guest at the 7-day mark and again at the 30-day mark and each would be lower than the "Nightly" rate. Thus, we are giving the guest a volume discount so to speak.

If you decide to encourage people to stay for longer periods of time, set the discounted "Weekly" rate at something that makes sense for both you (as far as your desired income) and the guest (as far as affordability).

Let's look at the regular "Weekly" rate with no discount. At $25 per night times 7 nights in a week, we make $175. If we give them a 10% discount, the weekly rate would be set at $158. Assuming an average of 4 weeks in a month, your monthly income would be $632.

What would a "Monthly" discount rate look like? If we take off another 10% we get: $632 − 10% = $569 per month. Not bad, right?

These are just some ideas to spark your creativity. There are no hard and fast rules for pricing. I chose a 10% discount randomly. And, you do not have to give a price break at all if you do not want to. If that is the case, just set the "Nightly" rate and leave the "Weekly" and "Monthly" rates blank.

In addition, you can increase the price by the number of guests if you wish. Scroll down to the "Additional Guests" section. Enter the additional amount per person per night that you want to charge after a certain number of guests. For example, your basic nightly rate is for 1 room for up to 2 people at $25 per night and a group of 4 people wants to rent the room. You could set the "Additional Guests" rate at $5 per night per guest after the first 2 guests. For this group of 4 people, the room would then be $35 per night. (First 2 guests at a regular flat rate of $25 per night, plus 2 guests at $5 each per night = $25 + $10 = $35 per night).

You have complete control over the pricing of your listing. If Weekly, Nightly and Monthly isn't specific enough for you, click on over to the "Advanced" Pricing and Terms tab where the price can be set differently for weekdays versus weekends, seasonally, or even daily if you like. How cool is that?! These prices will appear on your calendar so guests can see at a glance what the rates are for their particular dates so they can plan their trip accordingly.

Once you have all of your pricing set just the way you want it, save your changes and then click over to a very cool feature; the "Tools" tab. It is the third tab at the top. Here you can test out the pricing to be sure it works. Play with different date ranges to see what a guest would pay based on the rules you have set. I can see dollar signs in your eyes already!

Additional Fees

A couple of other charges to consider adding are cleaning fees and a security deposit.

Yes, believe it or not, you can also add a cleaning fee! Imagine, now you can get paid to clean your own house. Hallelujah! Keep in mind though that this may be a deterrent to some potential guests. If you do plan to add a fee, make it reasonable so as not to price yourself out of the market.

If you will be renting out an entire home or yacht, you may want to collect a security deposit up front as well. This will be returned to the guest after they check out, as long as there is no claim filed. If you need to file a claim, you have up to 48 hours to do so.

For added security and peace of mind, airbnb also provides hosts with $1,000,000 worth of protection against theft and vandalism. What could be better?

Terms

We have covered the pricing, now for the terms. If you go back to the Basic tab of the Pricing and Terms page, scroll down to the last section called, "Terms".

It is a fact of life that plans change. As hosts, we need to be able accommodate our guests' requests when they need to cancel a reservation or leave a bit early. To be fair though, we know that you have set aside the room for a particular guest and if they should cancel on short notice, that means you might be missing out on potential revenue. So airbnb provides three cancellation levels to choose from: Flexible, Moderate or Strict. If your cancellation policy is Flexible and the guest sends a request to cancel 24 hours prior to the beginning of their stay, they receive a full refund. If your cancellation policy is Moderate and the guest sends a request to cancel 5 days prior to the beginning of their stay, they receive a full refund. If your cancellation policy is Strict and the guest sends a request to cancel up to one week before their stay, they will receive a 50% refund. From the drop down menu, select which level you are most comfortable with: Flexible, Moderate or Strict.

House Rules

The House Rules are like a welcome letter with some do's and don'ts for your guests. Include any and all rules that come to mind. It might be as short as saying, "The only rule when you stay with us is there are no rules!" Or, you might want to list things such as, don't wear shoes in the house, no smoking, no drinking, no drugs, no fun...what have you. The House Rules differ from the House Manual in that they are shown to guests *before* they book a stay. If, for instance, the guest is a smoker and your House

Rules say, "No Smoking," this is where they would find that critical information.

Minimum and Maximum Length of Stay

Before we finish with the Pricing and Terms section, we need to consider two last things. First of all what is the shortest stay you will consider? It may be one day, two days, a week, a monthly sublet or a 1-year term. Also consider the longest amount of time you would like someone to stay with you. You may not want to limit this at all, it's up to you.

Lastly, set the check in and checkout time. Keep in mind that if one guest's stay ends on the same day another's begins, you will need some time in between to tidy up the place for the new guest. I recommend setting them at least an hour apart to give yourself enough time to change the bedding, sweep and mop (or vacuum), dust, wipe off surfaces, empty the trash and set a mint gingerly on the pillow, or any other nice little value-added gifts you provide for your guests.

Once you've set your times, you're done! Click Save.

Good job! You are ready to activate your listing.

10 ACTIVATING YOUR LISTING

And now for the shortest and simplest chapter. Drum roll please…. Click and slide the icon beside the word, "Hidden" to the left. It will turn green and read, "Visible".

Congratulations! You are officially open for business.

11 GREETINGS THAT WIN GUESTS

Now the inquiries will start flowing in. Keep in mind that the guests may be shopping around for the best place to stay in your area so you want to wow them with your warmth and kindness. Stand out from the rest by answering inquiries quickly! Within an hour is ideal. Answer warmly, "Hello, (insert first name here)!"

Then you can say something like, "We would be delighted to have you stay with us."

Answer any questions they might have in the most transparent, honest and positive manner possible.

You can add at the end, " I will pre-approve you for the nights you have requested and I look forward to meeting you soon."

Or something witty like, "We'll leave the light on for you!"

12 ACCEPTING A RESERVATION REQUEST

Once you receive a Reservation Request, you have 24 hours to answer it before it expires and the guest moves on to another host. You will have three options: Accept, Decline or Discuss More.

If you want to accept it, simply click on the radio button beside that choice. A window will open if you would like to include a message to the guest. VERY IMPORTANT, you must then click the box beside the Terms of Service disclaimer before clicking on the "Send" button or the reservation will not be locked in. If you have done it correctly, there will be a green button that says "ACCEPTED" next to your message string in the Inbox for that guest. Your calendar will also be automatically updated to show those dates as no longer available.

If for any reason, the terms of the guest's stay are incorrect, you can also go in and correct them by using the Special Offer feature which appears right below the text message box. Here you can change the dates, the number of guests and/or the total price for the stay. This can be a powerful marketing tool if you want to entice folks with a discount too.

13 WELCOMING A NEW GUEST

Did I just hear a taxi pull up outside? Is that a knock at the door? Congratulations, your first guest has arrived! After so many emails back and forth, reading their profile and seeing their picture, they are practically like family by now. Greet them with a warm welcome.

Invite them in. Offer to help carry their bags. Instruct them whether to take their shoes off or not before coming in the house. They will probably be tired from their long journey so be courteous and show them to their room first. You can give a brief tour after they have dropped their bags off in their room and had a moment to freshen up.

Go over the house rules and show them all of the wonderful things your house has to offer. After the tour, their first question will probably be, "what is the wifi password?" Their second question will be about parking and/or transportation. This is a great time to provide them with any maps you have of the local area. Many guests like to explore the immediate neighborhood on foot. In an urban setting, you would be amazed at how easy it is to get turned around if you are not familiar with the area. By providing a simple detailed street map of your area with key points of interest, you will be adding huge value to your guest's experience.

This is a great time to provide them with any discount coupons to local attractions as well. Offer recommendations for fun places that they might like to go, whether it be a museum, amusement park, club or one of the Seven Wonders of the World. The best way to add value is to be a one-stop shop; a wealth of knowledge and helpful suggestions. Use your creativity to add as many special touches as you can, to make their stay with you memorable and better than any ordinary hotel they might have stayed at.

14 FREEDOM THROUGH HOSTING

You are now on your way to wealth through a successful home-based business in the hospitality industry. I pray that this program will help you to achieve financial freedom and allow you to follow your dreams.

Cheers!

15 BONUS SECTION

Hot Tip #1- Keyless Entry

Guests like to feel that their things are secure. Always provide them with a key to their room. After hosting for so many years, we have learned a few tricks. In the beginning we lost a good number of keys and spent lots of time having duplicates made. It didn't take long before we discovered a wonderful Schlage keypad door lock that you can program a code to unlock the door. The code can be changed from time to time and it holds up to 19 unique codes that can be distributed among different users.

Hot Tip #2-Bed Etiquette

To protect mattresses from stains, add a waterproof bed cover that also has a pillowtop so it not only will add protection but comfort as well. Some waterproof mattress covers are plasticy and make a lot of noise but there are some out there that are made from a softer material that is still water repellant. It is also good to protect your mattress with a vinyl covering to eliminate the problem of bed bugs.

Hot Tip #3 – Instant Bed & Breakfast

Take your hosting to the next level by providing a continental breakfast. It's easy to do and your guests will love it. A continental breakfast is simply a breakfast that doesn't require cooking. Put out some cereal or breakfast breads and fruit. Let guests know that milk and juice are in the refrigerator and they can help themselves. Put out the paper bowls, napkins, plastic utensils (for easy cleanup), cups and voila, you have an instant Bed and Breakfast!

Sometimes the breakfast bar can look a little messy when there are open cereal boxes, loaves of bread, assorted tea boxes, honey, Nutella, and plates all strewn about. I use dispensers and organizers as much as possible to keep it looking neat and more inviting, plus it is easier to maintain.

Hot Tip #4 – Tax Benefits Galore

Start thinking like a business owner. You will receive a 1099 form from airbnb at the end of the year and are expected to pay taxes on the income earned.

However, you are now running a home-based business which means that you get tax write offs! Consult your tax advisor to see how you can deduct expenses such as a portion of your electric bill, gas bill, water bill, internet bill, mileage and other business-related expenses.

ABOUT THE AUTHOR

Miss Sue and her husband, Jaime have lived in their Pico Rivera home for over twenty years. Their love for hosting began in the early 1990's and through it they have been blessed to meet the most amazing people in the world. Their two children grew up in this environment where they caught many life lessons such as always being open and willing to share what you have and accepting all people as individuals without prejudice.

Pay My Mortgage!

CONSULTATION SERVICES

Miss Sue is also available as a consultant to help set up your new business. Send an email to info@vacationrentalsinla.net to set up a personal visit

www.ingramcontent.com/pod-product-compliance
Lightning Source LLC
Chambersburg PA
CBHW071632170526
45166CB00003B/1300